THE ANCIENT GREEKS

JOHN MALAM

RSVP

RAINTREE
STECK-VAUGHN
P U B L I S H E R S
A Steck-Vaughn Company

Austin, Texas
www.steck-vaughn.com

HISTORY STARTS HERE!
The Ancient Greeks
OTHER TITLES IN THE SERIES
The Ancient Egyptians • The Ancient Romans • The Aztecs

Published by Raintree Steck-Vaughn Publishers,
an imprint of Steck-Vaughn Company

Library of Congress Cataloging-in-Publication Data
Malam, John.
The Ancient Greeks / John Malam.
     p.   cm.—(History starts here)
     Includes bibliographical references and index.
     Summary: Introduces the history, culture, and people of ancient
     Greece and examines its many contributions to the development
     of Western society.
     ISBN 0-7398-1350-1 (hard)
     0-7398-1823-6 (soft)
     1. Greece—History—To 146 B.C.—Juvenile literature.
     2. Greeks—Social life and customs—Juvenile literature.
     [1. Greece—History—To 146 B.C. 2. Greece—Civilization—To 146 B.C.]
     I. Title. II. Series.
     DF77.M286 2000
     938—dc21   99-32523

Printed in Italy. Bound in the United States.
1 2 3 4 5 6 7 8 9 0 04 03 02 01 00

Title page picture: A vase showing women making offerings to the gods

Picture acknowledgments:
AKG London Ltd: 6, 10, 14 (Erich Lessing), 15 (Alfons Rath), 22 (John Hios),
27 (Erich Lessing); Ancient Art and Architecture Collection 18 (R Sheridan),
23 (R Sheridan), 29 (M&J Lynch); British Museum 1, 17; CM Dixon: 7, 8, 13, 19, 21, 24,
25, 26, 28; Tony Stone Images: 4 (George Grigoriou), 9 (Mervyn Rees), 10–11
(George Grigoriou), 20 (Robert Everts).

Illustrations: Michael Posen

CONTENTS

WHO WERE THE GREEKS?

Greece is a country in the south of Europe. It is warm and sunny and is almost completely surrounded by sea. There are many rugged mountains. They run across the land in long lines, called ranges.

Because mountains cover much of Greece, the Greeks have always lived by the sea, where the land is flatter and easier to farm.

BULGARIA

MACEDONIA

ALBANIA

Mount Olympus

GREECE

Ionian Sea

Aegean Sea

Delphi

TURKEY

Mycenae

Athens

Olympia

Epidaurus

Mediterranean Sea

Knossos

CRETE

This map shows how the mainland part of Greece is joined to other countries in Europe. About 2,000 islands belong to Greece. Less than 200 of them have people living on them.

It was here, more than 4,000 years ago, that the ancient Greeks lived. They created one of the world's first important civilizations. Some of the things we have today, such as democracy, the theater, and the Olympic Games, were started years ago by the ancient Greeks.

THE BEGINNING OF GREECE

The Minoans and the Mycenaeans were the first two important groups of people who lived in Greece.

The Minoans lived on Crete and other islands nearby. They built palaces with many rooms. They farmed the land and fished and hunted. They also knew how to write. The Minoans had their own language, which was not Greek.

This Minoan picture shows people leaping over the back of a charging bull. This was a game that young Minoan men played.

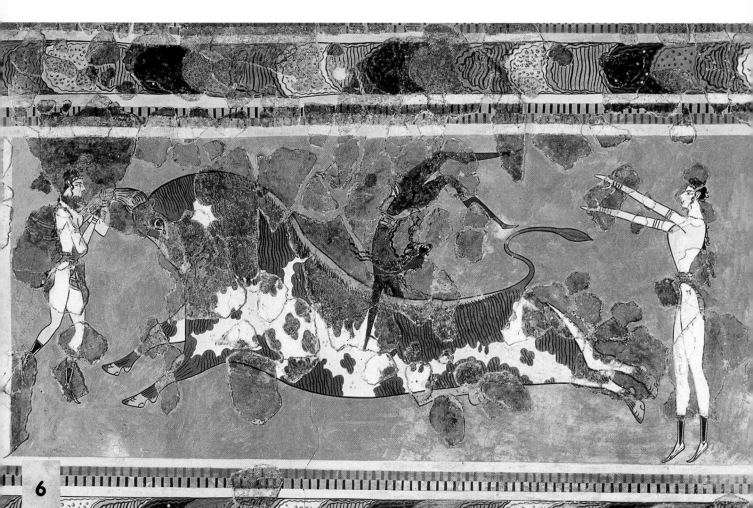

The city of Mycenae was built on top of a hill. Its strong walls protected the town from attackers. Above this gate are two stone lions.

A MYSTERIOUS END

Nobody knows how these two civilizations came to an end. Some people think that the great palaces of Minos were destroyed by an erupting volcano. Mycenae is thought to have disappeared because its people were at war with one another.

The Mycenaeans lived on the mainland. They lived in towns around the city of Mycenae and were ruled by kings. The Mycenaeans spoke a type of Greek. They are said to be the first Greeks.

The Minoans and the Mycenaeans lived about 4,000 years ago, and they traded with each other. The idea of writing spread from the Minoans to the Mycenaeans. Then, about 3,000 years ago, both civilizations came to an end.

ATHENS—CITY OF MARBLE

The Greeks who lived after the Mycenaeans built many towns and cities. One city, called Athens, became more powerful than all the rest.

Athens was at its most powerful about 2,500 years ago. It was a busy city. As many as 200,000 people lived there and in the countryside around. Athens owned valuable silver mines, and, like other Greek cities, had its own army. It had a fleet of warships, too.

Pericles was a great leader in Athens. He ordered the Parthenon to be built.

On top of a high hill stood a group of beautiful temples. They were built from white marble, which is a hard stone. The grandest temple of all was the Parthenon.

The Parthenon was once painted in bright colors, but the paint has worn away. It was built to honor the goddess Athena.

HOW A CITY WAS RUN

The ancient Greeks developed a form of government called democracy. This means "power by the people." It was a fair system because the citizens of Greece could decide how they wanted their city to be run.

An unpopular man could be sent away from the city if the citizens of Athens voted for him to go. They voted on pieces of broken pottery, called *ostraka*.

In Athens citizens held their meetings in the open air on the Pnyx, a hill. Its name meant "packing place."

Greek citizens chose their own leaders, made laws, and decided whether or not to go to war. Citizens were men born in the city whose parents had been born there, too. It did not matter if they were rich or poor.

GREEK CITIZENS

Only some people were allowed to be citizens of the city where they lived. Women, slaves, and most men from other Greek cities or foreign lands could not be citizens.

LIFE IN ANCIENT GREECE

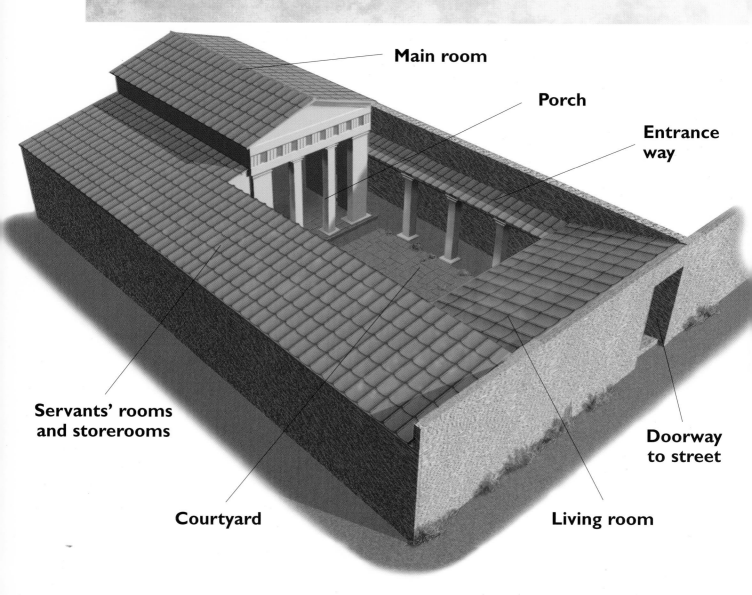

Main room

Porch

Entrance way

Servants' rooms and storerooms

Doorway to street

Courtyard

Living room

This is how a Greek house might have looked. Everyday life centered around the courtyard. This was where children played, where food was cooked, and where visitors were met.

People lived in houses built from clay bricks. Walls were painted white to keep the heat of the sun out. Houses had several rooms, placed around a courtyard. There were separate rooms for women, men, guests, and slaves. The main room was for feasting and entertaining guests.

A woman was expected to stay at home and look after the household. She cooked, cleaned, and cared for the children. She made the family's clothes. If the family had slaves, she gave them orders.

Men were free to come and go from the house as they wished. They went to work, bought food in the market square, and visited temples and festivals.

This woman is spinning wool to make cloth.

CHILDREN AND SCHOOL

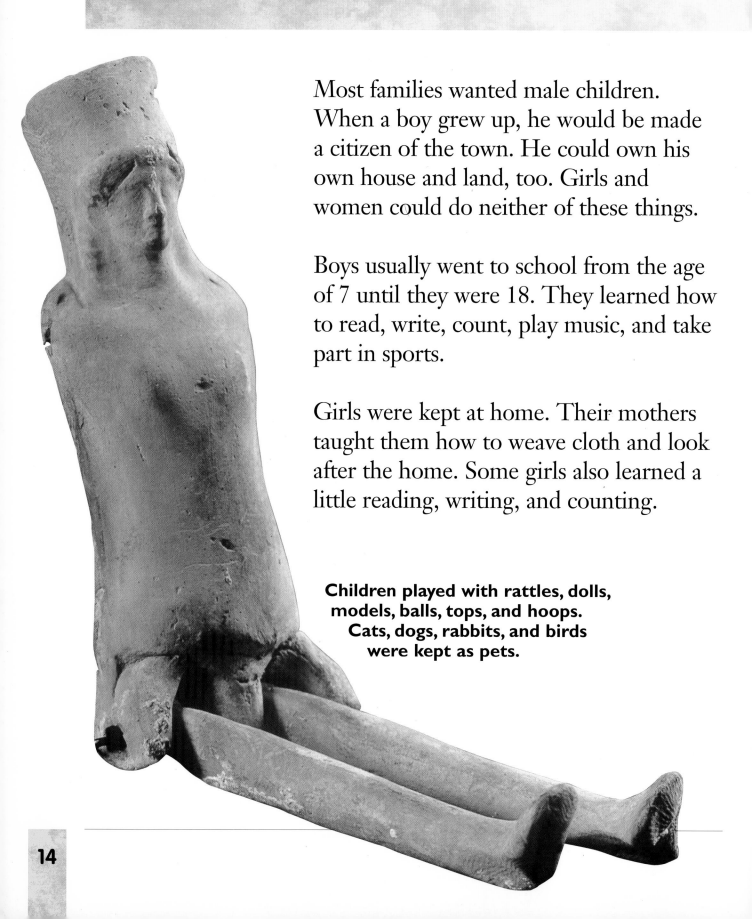

Most families wanted male children. When a boy grew up, he would be made a citizen of the town. He could own his own house and land, too. Girls and women could do neither of these things.

Boys usually went to school from the age of 7 until they were 18. They learned how to read, write, count, play music, and take part in sports.

Girls were kept at home. Their mothers taught them how to weave cloth and look after the home. Some girls also learned a little reading, writing, and counting.

Children played with rattles, dolls, models, balls, tops, and hoops. Cats, dogs, rabbits, and birds were kept as pets.

There were 24 letters in the Greek alphabet. The word *alphabet* comes from the names of the first two Greek letters, *alpha* and *beta*.

GREEK CLOTHES

Warm clothes were woven from sheep's wool. The flax plant was used to make linen, which was thinner and lighter than wool.

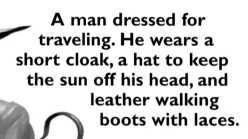

A man dressed for traveling. He wears a short cloak, a hat to keep the sun off his head, and leather walking boots with laces.

DYES

Clothes were usually left a natural creamy-white color. Sometimes dyes were used. Yellow dye was made from part of the crocus flower. Red came from the leaves of the madder plant. Purple came from the crushed shells of sea snails.

A lot of cloth was used in Greek clothes, which hung in neat, loose folds from the shoulders and waist.

Many people had short hair. If a woman had long hair, she might tie it up with ribbons.

Most Greek clothes were made from rectangular-shaped material. The material was draped around the body, and pins, brooches, and belts fastened it in place. Men, women, and children wore similar styles of clothing.

FOOD AND DRINK

Bread, cakes, and porridge were the main foods eaten by everyone. They were all made from barley, which grew in Greece.

This painting on a vase shows olives being knocked from a tree with sticks. Oil was squeezed from olives, which grew well in Greece. It was used in cooking and in lamps where it was burned to give light.

Farmers grew vegetables in their fields and sold them in the town's market square. They grew beans, peas, lentils, cabbages, cucumbers, lettuces, leeks, onions, and garlic. They gathered walnuts, chestnuts, and hazelnuts. Fruit crops were apples, pears, olives, grapes, dates, and figs.

The Greeks ate meat from sheep, pigs, cattle, and birds, as well as fish.

Most feasts were for men only. They ate and drank in the main room of the house, while lying on couches.

GODS AND GODDESSES

The ancient Greeks had many gods. Because people wanted the gods to protect and help them, they gave them presents. Some gave gifts of food and wine. The greatest gift was an animal, such as a sheep or a goat. It was killed by a priest, and prayers were offered.

People thought their wishes would be granted if the gifts pleased the gods. Farmers prayed for good harvests. Travelers prayed for safe journeys, and the sick prayed for good health.

The Greeks built great temples to please their gods. People from all over Greece went to this temple at Delphi to pray to Apollo, the god of healing.

20

This is Poseidon, the god of the sea. Statues often show him holding a three-pronged fish spear, called a trident.

Poseidon was a brother of Zeus, the king of the gods. Zeus was the god of weather. Statues often show him throwing a thunderbolt.

FESTIVALS AND GAMES

At a festival people relaxed and enjoyed themselves. It was a time to celebrate and give thanks to the gods. Colorful processions marked special occasions.

Sports festivals were always popular. The greatest of all was the Olympic Games. This took place once every four years at Olympia. The festival lasted five days.

It was at the racetrack in Olympia that most of the events took place. The pentathlon included five different types of athletic events that each competitor had to enter.

Athletes in ancient Greece did not wear clothes. The paintings on this vase show athletes being presented with prizes at the games.

Men from all parts of Greece, and from overseas, too, went to Olympia to take part in the games. Women were not allowed to go there. A winning athlete was given a crown of olive branches or laurel. He brought honor to his city by winning at the games.

STORIES AND THEATER

Stories were a part of everyday life in Greece. Storytellers, or bards, learned stories by heart, then told them from memory. Crowds gathered to listen.

Homer was a poet who told many popular stories. He may have been blind.

You can see from this theater at Epidaurus how the audience sat in the open air on stone seats. Plays were performed in the daytime.

People liked to go to the theater. Actors wore masks and costumes and put on lots of different plays. All the actors were men. Some plays were funny, and some were serious. They were usually set in the past and told stories about gods and heroes.

THE GREEKS AT WAR

The Greeks fought many battles. Greek city-states argued and fought wars with each other as well as with other countries.

The Greeks went to war with the Persians, who wanted to invade Greece. The Athenians were led by a great commander, Themistocles. At Salamis they fought a great sea battle. The Persians lost about 300 ships and were beaten.

Greek warships had battering rams. They smashed into enemy ships and made big holes in their wooden sides to sink them.

Greek soldiers fought
with swords and long
spears. They wore
armor to protect their
bodies.

THE END OF THE GREEKS

Alexander the Great, king of Macedonia, became ruler of all Greece. His empire controlled lands from Greece to India and Egypt. After Alexander died, his empire was split up into smaller parts. Greece became less powerful.

Many years later the Romans came from Italy, to the west of Greece. They built a powerful empire of their own. Greece became part of it.

Alexander was a hero. Because he was such a great leader, he became known as Alexander the Great.

The Romans built this temple in France. It was copied from the style of temples the Greeks built.

The ancient Greeks have taught us many things. Their influence can still be seen today in our art, in our sports, and in the way many countries are governed.

THE ROMANS
The Romans liked the Greeks and the way they lived. They admired the style of their buildings, which they copied, and they based their alphabet on the Greek alphabet. They also enjoyed Greek plays and poetry.

IMPORTANT DATES

All the dates in this list are B.C. dates. This stands for "Before Christ." B.C. dates are counted back from the year 0, which is the year we say Jesus Christ was born. Some dates have the letter *c.* in front of them. This stands for *circa*, which means "about." These dates are guesses, because no one knows what the exact date is.

c. 2000 B.C. The first Greek-speaking people arrived on mainland Greece.

c. 2000 B.C. The Minoans built palaces on Crete.

c. 1900 B.C. The Mycenaeans built towns on mainland Greece.

1600 B.C. Mycenae flourished.

c. 1400 B.C. The first Greek writing was developed. The town of Mycenae was at its greatest.

c. 1200 B.C. The traditional date of the Trojan War.

c.1100 B.C. The Minoan and Mycenaean civilizations came to an end.

800–500 B.C. The Archaic Period, the time when ancient Greece began to expand and grow rich.

c. 800 B.C. The Greeks develop their own language.

c. 800 B.C. Homer, the greatest Greek poet, lived.

776 B.C. The first Olympic Games were held.

753 B.C. Rome was founded.

c. 600 B.C. Greek poetry became very famous.

534 B.C. The first Greek tragedy was performed.

500–336 B.C. The Classical Age, the period when Athens went to war with the Persians.

c. 500 B.C. Democracy was introduced in Athens.

490 B.C. The Greeks beat the Persians in a battle on land, at Marathon.

480 B.C. The Greeks beat the Persians in a battle at sea, at Salamis.

479–431 B.C. The Golden Age, the period when Athens became wealthy and powerful.

c. 460–429 B.C. Pericles was leader of Athens.

447–438 B.C. The Parthenon was built in Athens.

431–404 B.C. Athens lost a war with Greek rival city-state, Sparta.

430 B.C. Plague in Athens.

359–336 B.C. The reign of King Philip II, of Macedonia.

338 B.C. King Philip II conquered and became the ruler of Greece.

336 B.C. King Philip II died. His son, Alexander, became king.

331 B.C. Alexander defeats Persians at battle of Gaugamela.

327 B.C. Alexander's army invaded India.

323 B.C. Alexander died, and his empire broke apart.

146 B.C. Greece became part of the Roman Empire.

GLOSSARY

Bard Another name for a storyteller.

Citizen A Greek who was born a free man and who had a say in how he wanted his town to be run.

Democracy A type of government in which ordinary people have a say in how they want things to be done.

Marble A hard white or colored stone.

Minoans A group of people who lived on Crete and other islands nearby.

Mycenaeans A group of people who lived mostly on the mainland of Greece.

Olympians The name given to the family of 12 major gods and goddesses.

Olympic Games The festival of contests in sports, music, and poetry, held every four years.

Olympus, Mount A mountain in northern Greece, believed to be where the gods lived.

Persians People who lived in Persia, now called Iran.

Poseidon The god of the sea.

Servant Someone who works for another person.

Slave Someone who is owned by another person.

Zeus The king of the gods. He was the god of weather.

FURTHER INFORMATION

BOOKS TO READ

Crosher, Judith. *Technology in the Time of Ancient Greece* (Technology in the Time of.) Austin, TX: Raintree Steck-Vaughn, 1998.

Steele, Philip and Anton Powell. *The Greek News*. Cambridge, MA: Candlewick Press, 1996.

Steele, Philip. *Clothes and Crafts of Ancient Greece*. New York: Dillon Press, 1998.

INDEX